Sara Swan Miller

Moles and Hedgehogs

What They Have in Common

Franklin Watts - A Division of Grolier Publishing
New York • London • Hong Kong • Sydney • Danbury, Connecticut

For Lani again
You can learn to love these guys too!

Photographs ©: Animals Animals: 31 (Stephen Dalton), 33 (Michael Fogden); BBC Natural History Unit: 1 (Niall Benvie), 41 (Simon King), 38, 39 (Pete Oxford); Dembinsky Photo Assoc.: 7, 19 (Gary Meszaros); Dwight R. Kuhn Photography: 13; NHPA: 29 (John Hartley), 35, 42 (Daniel Heuclin); Peter Arnold Inc.: 24, 25 (Fred Bruemer), 6 (Hans Pfletschinger), 43 (Carl R. Sams II), 26, 27, 37 (Roland Seitre); Photo Researchers: 5 bottom left (Stephen Dalton), 5 top right (Sturgis McKeever), cover (Rod Planck), 14, 15 (Leonard Lee Rue), 21 (N. Smythe), 5 bottom right (Howard Uible), 23 (Martin Wendler/Okapia); Visuals Unlimited: 40 top (Jeff J. Daly), 5 top left (Leonard Lee Rue), 16, 17 (Rob & Ann Simpson), 40 bottom (John Sohlden).

Illustrations by Jose Gonzales and Steve Savage

The photo on the cover shows a star-nosed mole. The photo on the title page shows a hedgehog searching for food.

Visit Franklin Watts on the Internet at:
http://publishing.grolier.com

Library of Congress Cataloging-in-Publication Data

Miller, Sara Swan.
Moles and hedgehogs: what they have in common / Sara Swan Miller
    p. cm. — (Animals in order)
  Includes bibliographical references and index.
  Summary: Discusses the characteristics of mammals known as insectivores, including hedgehogs, tenrecs, shrews, desmens, moles, and solenodons.
    ISBN 0-531-11633-6 (lib. bdg.)   0-531-13957-3 (pbk.)
    1. Insectivora—Juvenile literature. [1. Insectivores.] I. Title. II. Series.
QL737.I5 M56   2001
599.33—dc21   99-057533

Contents

What Is an Insectivore?

Have you ever seen a small furry animal scuffling in dead leaves at night? Did you think it was a mouse? It might have been a shrew. Have you seen mole tunnels in your lawn? Maybe you have watched a prickly hedgehog waddling along under a row of bushes.

You might think these small animals are closely related to mice and rats. Mice and rats belong to a group of animals called rodents. All rodents can be identified by their teeth. Moles, shrews, and hedgehogs have a different kind of teeth, so they are not rodents. Instead, they belong to a group, or *order*, of animals called *insectivores* (in-SEK-tih-vohrz). The word "insectivore" means "insect-eater." Moles, hedgehogs, shrews, and all the other animals in this group eat insects.

Look at the four insectivores on the next page. Can you guess all the things they have in common?

Eastern mole

Least shrew

European hedgehog

Streaked tenrec

Traits of the Insectivores

You probably noticed a few things right away. All insectivores are small and furry. Each one has a pointed nose and small eyes, and they all walk with their feet planted fully on the ground, as a bear or a person does.

Insectivores do look a lot like rats and mice, but if you compare the teeth of a mouse and a mole, you will see that they are quite different. A mouse has a gap between its *incisors*, or front teeth, and its *cheek teeth*. A mole has teeth all along its jaws, including pointed *canine teeth*, which are good for tearing up *prey*.

Scientists can also decide whether an animal is an insectivore by studying the bones in its head. Some of the bones that most *mammals* have are missing in insectivores. Other bones are smaller or not complete. You would need X-ray eyes to see *those* things!

Insectivores are the descendants of mammals that lived when dinosaurs still roamed Earth. The insect-eaters survived because they

This hedgehog is using its teeth to eat a cricket.

were so small. Dinosaurs probably didn't pay much attention to them. Because they had fur and were warm-blooded, insectivores could come out at night when the air was too cold for dinosaurs. Plenty of insects lived millions of years ago, so these small mammals had plenty to eat.

Insectivores haven't changed much since the days of the dinosaurs. Most insect-eaters still come out at night and sleep during the day. They still eat mostly insects, but some eat other small animals too. Insectivores can't see very well, so they depend on their sense of smell to find prey.

Insectivores have also stayed small. One of the largest insectivores in the world is the common tenrec. It's about the size of a house cat. The smallest insectivore, a tiny shrew, weighs a little more than a penny!

This smokey shrew is eating a snake.

The Order of Living Things

A tiger has more in common with a house cat than with a daisy. A true bug is more like a butterfly than a jellyfish. Scientists arrange living things into groups based on how they look and how they act. A tiger and a house cat belong to the same group, but a daisy belongs to a different group.

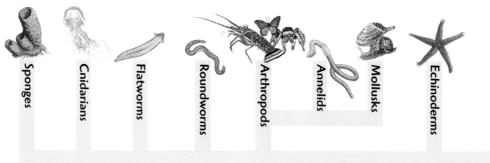

Sponges · Cnidarians · Flatworms · Roundworms · Arthropods · Annelids · Mollusks · Echinoderms

Animals

Plants · Fungi

Protists

Monerans

All living things can be placed in one of five groups called *kingdoms*: the plant kingdom, the animal kingdom, the fungus kingdom, the moneran kingdom, or the protist kingdom. You can probably name many of the creatures in the plant and animal kingdoms. The fungus kingdom includes mushrooms, yeasts, and molds. The moneran and protist kingdoms contain thousands of living things that are too small to see without a microscope.

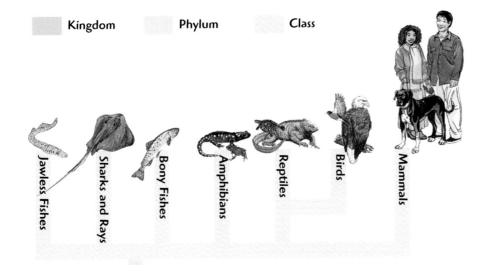

Kingdom Phylum Class

Jawless Fishes
Sharks and Rays
Bony Fishes
Amphibians
Reptiles
Birds
Mammals

Chordates

Because there are millions and millions of living things on Earth, some of the members of one kingdom may not seem all that similar. The animal kingdom includes creatures as different as tarantulas and trout, jellyfish and jaguars, salamanders and sparrows, elephants and earthworms.

To show that an elephant is more like a jaguar than an earthworm, scientists further separate the creatures in each kingdom into more specific groups. The animal kingdom can be divided into nine *phyla*. Humans belong to the chordate phylum. Almost all chordates have a backbone.

Each phylum can be subdivided into many *classes*. Humans, mice, and elephants all belong to the mammal class. Each class can be further divided into orders; orders into *families*, families into *genera*, and genera into *species*. All the members of a species are very similar.

9

How Insectivores Fit In

You can probably guess that the insectivores belong to the animal kingdom. They have much more in common with bees and bats than with maple trees and morning glories.

Insectivores belong to the chordate phylum. Almost all chordates have a backbone and a skeleton. Can you think of other chordates? Examples include lions, mice, snakes, birds, fish, and whales.

The chordate phylum can be divided into several classes. Insectivores belong to the mammal class. Mice, whales, dogs, cats, and humans are all mammals.

There are seventeen orders of mammals. The insectivores make up one of these orders. As you learned earlier, insectivores eat mostly insects, but many species enjoy a variety of other foods, including small animals and plants.

The insectivores are divided into a number of families and genera. There are 6 living families and more than 375 different species. Shrews are the largest family, with more than 300 species.

Insectivores live almost everywhere on Earth, except Australia and the polar ice caps. Some spend most of their time underground, while others spend most of their time in the water. A few prefer to live in trees. Read on to learn more about fourteen species of these little-known animals.

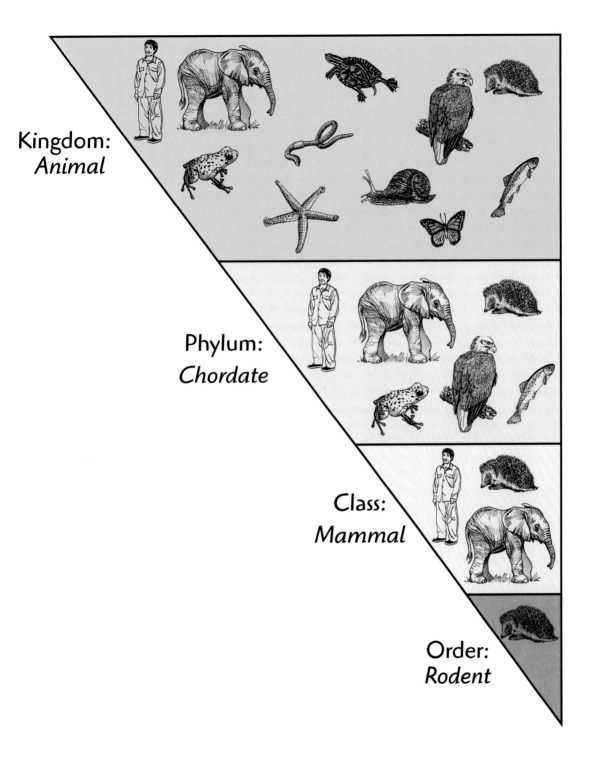

Kingdom: *Animal*

Phylum: *Chordate*

Class: *Mammal*

Order: *Rodent*

Moles

FAMILY: Talpidae
COMMON EXAMPLE: Star-nosed mole
GENUS AND SPECIES: *Condylura cristata*
SIZE: 4 to 5 inches (10 to 13 cm)

In a dark tunnel underground, a hungry star-nosed mole digs along with its large, strong front feet. It feels its way with the ring of fleshy feelers on its nose. Suddenly, the mole senses an earthworm. The mole grabs the worm with its sharp front teeth and gobbles it down.

The pink feelers around the mole's nose help the animal hunt for its food. A star-nosed mole wiggles its nose constantly, and the feelers pick up electric fields around the small creatures the mole eats. This helps the mole find its prey in the dark.

Star-nosed moles are well adapted for life in damp tunnels. Their velvety fur is waterproof and lies comfortably in any direction. That makes it easy for moles to move both forward and backward in their tunnels. Their large, sharp-clawed front feet make them powerful diggers.

Star-nosed moles are also strong swimmers. Their tunnels often end in ponds and streams where they swim quickly about, hunting water insects, small shrimp, and fish.

Moles have to keep eating almost all the time. They hunt day and night throughout the year. Nothing keeps them from their constant search for food, not even snow and ice.

Moles

FAMILY: Talpidae
COMMON EXAMPLE: Eastern mole
GENUS AND SPECIES: *Scalopus aquaticus*
SIZE: 4 to 6 1/2 inches (10 to 17 cm)

Like the star-nosed mole, the eastern mole is a real live eating machine. Although it eats almost constantly, an eastern mole is busier at some hours than at others. This animal does most of its work between eight o'clock in the morning and four o'clock in the afternoon. It usually hunts some more between eleven o'clock at night and four o'clock in the morning. Even an eastern mole has to rest sometimes!

These moles make their tunnels in moist or sandy soil that is easy to dig. Some tunnels are deep and end in a *burrow*. Others lie close to the surface, where the moles can find worms and insects to eat.

When an eastern mole digs, it looks as if it is diving into the dirt. It pushes its wide front feet into the soil and follows with its head and shoulders. Then it thrusts its front feet back and flings the loose soil behind it. The webbing between

14

the animal's toes lets the mole use its feet like small shovels. An eastern mole can dig up to 14 1/2 feet (4.5 m) in an hour.

If you look for an eastern mole's eyes, you won't find them. It doesn't need eyes in the darkness underground. Instead, it has very simple sense organs that can detect light. You'll also have trouble finding this animal's ears. It depends on its sharp sense of smell.

Shrews

FAMILY: *Soricidae*
COMMON EXAMPLE: Least shrew
GENUS AND SPECIES: *Cryptotis parva*
SIZE: 2 1/2 to 3 inches (6 to 8 cm)

The least shrew may be tiny, but it is fierce. It runs around day and night, pouncing on any small animal it can find. The shrew usually snatches up insects, worms, or snails, but it will even grab a small mouse if one crosses its path. When it catches a grasshopper, the shrew tears the insect open, eats its soft insides, and leaves the tough skin behind.

Every day a least shrew eats its own weight in food. You would have to eat about 200 hamburgers to do that! If a least shrew goes for more than 3 or 4 hours without eating, it will die of hunger.

Unlike other shrews, least shrews seem to enjoy one another's company. As many as thirty may curl up together in the same underground nest. Some-times least shrews help one another dig their burrows and nests. They will even share the same piece of food without fighting.

Least shrews in the southern United States often give birth several times a year. They may have as many as nine babies at a time. The young grow quickly and are ready to leave the nest in only 3 weeks. About 10 days later, the young shrews are ready to have their own babies. That's a lot of shrews coming into the world every year!

So why haven't shrews taken over the world? Most of them don't live long enough. The woods are full of enemies, from owls to foxes to cats.

Shrews

FAMILY: *Soricidae*
COMMON EXAMPLE: Masked shrew
GENUS AND SPECIES: *Sorex cinereus*
SIZE: 3 1/2 to 4 inches (9 to 10 cm)

A tiny masked shrew scurries quickly along a mouse trail, searching for something to eat. That usually means anything it can find. Here's a grasshopper! There's a beetle—and a moth! The shrew devours them all quickly and races onward, looking for more food.

Like other shrews, a masked shrew has to eat almost all the time to fuel its "engine." Your heart beats about 70 to 90 times a minute, but a masked shrew's heart beats 600 to 800 times a minute. When something frightens the animal, its heart can beat up to 1,200 times a minute!

Masked shrews live in the United States and Canada. They don't have a thick layer of fat or thick hair to keep them warm. How do these little animals survive in the winter? They tunnel under the snow. The snow acts as a blanket, protecting the masked shrew from the harsh wind and cold air. In the summer, masked shrews find shelter under damp leaves.

Masked shrews live alone most of the time, except during mating season. Each one has its own home range where it feeds and nests. If a stranger comes, a masked shrew will run at it, squeaking madly. If the intruder doesn't run away, the shrew attacks!

Solenodons

FAMILY: Solenodontidae
EXAMPLE: Haitian solenodon
GENUS AND SPECIES: *Solenodon paradoxus*
SIZE: 12 inches (30 cm)

Dusk falls in a forest in Haiti, and the solenodons begin to wake up. All day, these shrewlike animals sleep together in a big pile inside a hollow log. Nighttime is hunting time. One by one, they climb out of the log and begin to waddle along the forest floor.

Solenodons are awkward animals. They run in a clumsy zigzag pattern. People who have seen them move say they cannot walk in a straight line. If something frightens a solenodon and it tries to run away, the animal often trips over its own toes. It may even tumble head over heels. When this animal gets going, however, it can run very fast. It can also climb trees.

Solenodons eat just about anything that comes their way— insects, worms, snails, and even small reptiles or chickens. They have poisonous spit, or *saliva*, so they can kill large prey. Solenodons use their long noses to dig up grubs and roots. Their strong claws help them rip open rotten logs and search for insects. Sometimes they eat fruit and other plant parts.

Because solenodons eat so many different things, you might expect them to be very successful. After all, they have been around for millions of years. Now, however, solenodons are becoming quite

20

rare. They live only on the islands of Cuba and Haiti. Although they have few natural enemies, the clumsy animals are often killed by pet dogs and cats.

Hedgehogs

FAMILY: Erinaceidae
COMMON EXAMPLE: European hedgehog
GENUS AND SPECIES: *Erinaceus europaeus*
SIZE: 7 1/2 to 10 inches (19 to 25 cm)

A prickly hedgehog scuffles through a pile of dead leaves, searching for a meal. A fat beetle tries to scuttle away from those hungry jaws, but the hedgehog pounces and quickly crunches it up.

When the alert hedgehog spots a fox nearby, it curls up in a tight ball of prickles. The spines that cover the hedgehog's body are 2 to 3 inches (5 to 8 cm) long. The fox can't reach the hedgehog's soft belly. It gives up and trots away.

If the hedgehog had been near a pond, the story might have had a different ending. If the fox had rolled the hedgehog into water, it would have had to uncurl its body. Otherwise, it would drown. That's when the fox could have attacked.

Grown hedgehogs are safe from most *predators*, but their young are helpless. Newborns are deaf and blind. The soft white spines that cover their bodies cannot protect them. A few days after hedgehogs are born, their soft spines fall out and hard, dark spines grow in. In 2 months, the babies are ready to go out into the world.

Hedgehogs eat almost anything they can find, including insects, worms, mice, vegetables, and dead animals. Stinging wasps and bees don't bother them. Hedgehogs even eat poisonous snakes.

Hedgehogs

FAMILY: Erinaceidae

COMMON EXAMPLE: Long-eared desert
hedgehog

GENUS AND SPECIES: *Hemiechinus auritus*

SIZE: 4 1/2 to 10 1/2 inches (11 to 27 cm)

A desert hedgehog may look silly to you, with its big ears sticking out. Those ears help the animal survive in its harsh desert *habitat*. The ears give off heat and help keep the hedgehog cool in the hot desert air. They also help the animal pick up the tiny sounds made by insects and other prey.

Like its cousin the European hedgehog, a desert hedgehog will eat almost anything. It likes beetles, grasshoppers, and other insects best, but it will also gobble up eggs, fruit, and vegetables. It will even eat scorpions, lizards, and small snakes. Finding food and water in the desert can be difficult, but this hedgehog is a tough little creature. It can go for as long as 10 weeks without eating or drinking.

Desert hedgehogs keep to themselves most of the time. During the day, they curl up in the burrows and rest. In the evening, they come out to hunt for food. They may wander as far as 5 1/2 miles (9 km) in a single night.

24

A female desert hedgehog has young only once a year. Her *litter* contains no more than four babies. The newborns are helpless. They have only a few short, soft spines on their naked bodies. Within a few hours, the spines harden and grow four times longer. Two weeks later, the babies are covered with hard spines. Other animals leave hedgehogs alone after they grow hard spines!

Gymnures

FAMILY: Erinaceidae
COMMON EXAMPLE: Moon rat
GENUS AND SPECIES: *Echinosorex gymnurus*
SIZE: 10 to 18 inches (25 to 46 cm)

A moon rat isn't really a rat. It is a cousin of the hedgehog, but it doesn't have spines. Instead, a moon rat's body is covered with thick fur. That's why some people call them furry hedgehogs.

Even though a moon rat has no spines on its body, it can defend itself from enemies. If a coyote or fox attacks, the moon rat gives off a horrible smell. Not even the hungriest predator wants to eat anything that stinky!

The moon rat has a long, flexible nose that helps it sniff out all kinds of good things to eat. It sneaks about in the undergrowth, hunting for insects, spiders, scorpions, and other small animals. Sometimes the moon rat climbs trees to munch on fruit. It's a good swimmer too. It dives into streams and ponds to catch crabs and *mollusks*. It may even snatch fish and frogs.

Moon rats live alone most of the time. When two moon rats meet, one usually hisses loudly at the other. If that doesn't drive the stranger away, the moon rat lets out a low, threatening roar.

Female moon rats have young twice a year. They mark the entrance to their nests with a scent from *glands* under their tails. The scent smells like rotten onions or ammonia. That sharp smell sends a warning message to enemies and other moon rats. Leave my babies alone!

Desmans

FAMILY: Talpidae

EXAMPLE: Russian desman

GENUS AND SPECIES: *Desmana moschata*

SIZE: 7 to 8 1/2 inches (18 to 22 cm)

If you ever have a chance to see a Russian desman swimming along in a pond, you might think it is a muskrat. Both animals have a long naked tail and webbed back feet. Like the muskrat, the Russian desman uses musk glands under its tail to mark its *territory*.

If you could compare the teeth of each animal, however, you would see a big difference. A muskrat is a rodent. Like mice and rats, it has a gap between its front teeth and its cheek teeth. A desman has a full set of insectivore teeth.

Unlike some insectivores, desmans often live in groups. As many as eight animals may share a den.

Although these animals dig burrows on land, they spend a lot of time in the water. They are well suited for life in ponds and streams. Their flat tails help them steer through water. The thick hair on the pads of their feet gives them an extra boost as they swim. Their fur has two layers—long, waterproof hairs on top and a warm, dense layer underneath.

Desmans spend the whole night hunting in the water. They probe the muddy bottom of their watery world with their long, sensitive snouts. They are feeling for water insects, snails, and shrimp. Their

sharp claws and teeth help them snatch up fish, frogs, and other water animals. When the sun begins to rise, desmans swim home to their burrows to sleep the day away.

Shrews

FAMILY: Soricidae
COMMON EXAMPLE: Eurasian water shrew
GENUS AND SPECIES: *Neomys fodiens*
SIZE: 2 1/2 to 3 1/2 inches (6 to 9 cm)

That animal swimming in the pond looks very much like a mouse, but mice don't swim. Water shrews do, though. Bristles on the underside of their tails and on their paws help them swim quite swiftly.

Like other shrews, water shrews have to eat almost constantly. All year long, they spend most of the day and night diving into the water to find food. They eat just about anything they can catch. They gobble up shrimp, snails, water striders, and insect *larvae*. Sometimes they go after larger prey, such as frogs, tadpoles, newts, and fish.

A water shrew has poisonous saliva. When it grabs a frog or a fish in its mouth, the poison paralyzes the prey so the shrew can eat it easily. Just a tiny bit of this poison can kill a mouse. If a shrew bit you, it would really hurt. Even if its teeth didn't break your skin, its saliva would burn you and keep on burning for days.

Female shrews have young several times a year. Each litter may have as many as twelve young. Water shrews need to have lots of young because they have so many enemies. In the water, large hungry fish hunt them. On land, foxes and weasels prey on shrews. Even if a shrew can escape all those predators, a silent owl may swoop down out of nowhere and snatch the shrew up in its claws.

Golden Moles

FAMILY: Chrysochloridae
COMMON EXAMPLE: Grant's golden mole
GENUS AND SPECIES: *Eremitalpa granti*
SIZE: 3 inches (8 cm)

If you ever see a golden mole, you will understand how it got its name. The dense fur on the mole's back has a greenish color. In bright sunlight, the fur seems to glow and shimmer. Some people in Africa collect golden mole skins. They think the skins bring good luck.

Even people in Africa don't see golden moles very often. Like a true mole, this animal spends most of its life underground. It digs just under the surface of the sand dunes where it lives, searching for worms, grubs, and beetles. The golden mole has very strong front feet with two long, strong claws that are perfect for digging through the sand. A tough, leathery pad on the mole's nose also helps it dig.

Golden moles come out of their burrows only on rainy nights. They know it is a good time to hunt for worms that have been flooded out. It's a good thing these moles have waterproof coats.

Golden moles can't see because skin covers their tiny eyes, but their excellent sense of smell helps them sniff out their prey. They also have special bones in their head that pick up vibrations. That's how they know when a predator is lurking. To escape from enemies, they quickly tunnel to safety.

Tenrecs

FAMILY: Tenrecidae
COMMON EXAMPLE: Streaked tenrec
GENUS AND SPECIES: *Hemicentetes semispinosus*
SIZE: 6 1/4 to 7 1/2 inches (16 to 19 cm)

A streaked tenrec rustles quietly along the forest floor, hunting for some juicy worms. It sticks its long, slender snout under the leaves, sniffing and feeling about. No worm is safe from a hungry tenrec!

Suddenly, the tenrec hears a sound. Danger! A mongoose is on the prowl! The tenrec can defend itself, though. It sticks up the sharp spines on its back and runs right at the mongoose, making noisy "crunch-crunch" sounds. The startled mongoose runs away, and the tenrec gets back to work.

Tenrecs can be noisy. When males fight over a female, they make their loud "crunch" noises and strange "putt-putt" sounds to scare each other. The rest of the time, however, tenrecs get along just fine. Together, they dig long burrows where they make nests to raise their young.

When a male tenrec has won his mate, the two stay together for several weeks. The female takes care of the young. She has an unusual way to keep track of them. She vibrates the quills on her back, making a sound a little like a cricket. The babies then quiver their own little quills to answer, "Here we are!"

Shrew Tenrecs

FAMILY: Tenrecidae
COMMON NAME: Long-tailed shrew tenrec
GENUS AND SPECIES: *Microgale nov*
SIZE: 2 1/2 to 4 inches (6 to 10 cm)

This animal's tail is sometimes longer than its body. That's why it's called "long-tailed." The little shrew tenrec looks a lot like a shrew. It acts like one too. It runs about at night, hunting for insects. If it comes across an ant nest, it digs it up and eats the ant eggs.

A shrew tenrec doesn't need to eat constantly like a true shrew does. It rests during the day and hunts only at night. If it finds plenty of food, the shrew tenrec gets fat. One captive animal weighed about as much as a jar of peanut butter. When a shrew tenrec gets that fat, it eats less and goes into a resting stage. If food is scarce, however, the shrew tenrec can get scrawny. It may weigh as little as a can of soup. Then it has to hunt constantly to build itself up again.

Shrew tenrecs have a lot to say to each other. When two strangers meet, they usually make soft, peaceful squeaking noises. When shrew tenrecs fight, they may try to scare each other with loud squeals. If that doesn't work, they start to scream. Shrew tenrecs also use smells to communicate. They mark their territories with musk from under their tails. When they groom themselves, they spread saliva over their face and paws. The smell helps shrew tenrecs recognize one another.

Tenrecs

FAMILY: Tenrecidae
COMMON EXAMPLE: Tail-less tenrec
GENUS AND SPECIES: *Tenrec ecaudatus*
SIZE: 10 1/2 to 15 1/4 inches (27 to 39 cm)

The tail-less tenrec, also called the common tenrec, is one of the largest insectivores. It is about the size of a pet cat. If an enemy finds this tenrec in its burrow, it raises the stiff mane on its back and opens its mouth wide. Its loud hisses, squeaks, squeals, and odd "piff piff" noises are usually enough to scare off an enemy.

Tail-less tenrecs like to live and hunt near water. They swim about in rice paddies or nose through the underbrush at night, searching for prey. Insects are their favorite food, but they also eat snakes, frogs, and small mammals. A hungry tenrec will even gobble up plants and fruit.

These tenrecs have long, sensitive whiskers on their snouts that help them find prey. Their whiskers and the long hairs on their back pick up vibrations in the air. They have better eyesight than most insectivores, and they are excellent hunters.

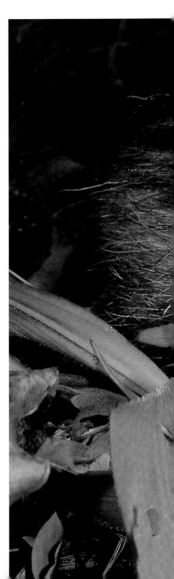

A female tail-less tenrec may have as many as thirty-two young in a single litter. No other mammal has so many young at once. At birth, the babies are blind and helpless. In about 3 weeks, however, the young begin following their mother through the underbrush as she searches for food. Imagine seeing lots and lots of baby tenrecs pattering along in a line!

Insectivores and People

Insectivores are so small and secretive that people don't think about them very much. The only insectivore most people have experience with is the mole. Many people complain about the holes and tunnels that moles dig in their lawns and gardens. Some people think the only good mole is a dead mole, and they find all kinds of ways to trap moles or drive them away.

A mole trap

The holes in this lawn were made by a mole.

A boy watches two pet hedgehogs eat.

Most of us don't realize how much good these busy little insect-eaters do. Without insectivores, insects would overrun our planet. Although mole tunnels can be annoying, maybe people should be grateful that moles keep pests away from their gardens.

Most of us ignore insectivores, but some people have found them useful. In the past, people trapped moles and desmans for their soft, dense fur and made perfume from the musk glands under a desman's tail. In Madagascar, people once hunted tenrecs for their meat. Today, many people keep hedgehogs as pets. Hedgehog lovers form clubs to keep in touch and share news and information.

Insectivores have been around for millions of years, and many species should be able to thrive for years to come. But other species are in trouble and could disappear forever. What is happening?

Human activities cause most of the problems. When people spray poisons to kill insects, moles and shrews suffer. They eat the insects, and the poisons build up in their bodies. After months of eating poisoned insects, the animals simply die.

In Asia, hunters killed so many desmans that very few are left. These animals have other troubles too. People have turned their habitats into cropland and housing developments. They have drained the wetlands where the desmans used to hunt for food. In some places, the water became so polluted that desmans couldn't live there. Many shrews and moles have the same problems. Water pollution, destroying habitats, and insect poisons hurt them all.

In some parts of the world, people have introduced new predators into the places where insectivores live. In Haiti, for instance, cats, dogs, and mongooses all prey on solenodons. Now it looks as though the clumsy, helpless solenodon is doomed.

This desman has just taken a swim.

This muskrat may look harmless, but it may mean trouble for a desman.

Desmans have a similar problem. When people brought muskrats and *nutria* to places where desmans live, the new animals ate the desmans' food and took over their homes. The desmans have had a hard time competing with the larger intruders.

As people build more highways and take over more animal habitats, insectivores have fewer places to live and find food. Highways are dangerous too. In Great Britain alone, speeding cars kill 100,000 hedgehogs every year!

Scientists are worried about insectivores. They know how important these animals are. Some scientists are trying to find out more about these secretive little animals so that people can figure out how to help them. Laws that protect insectivores and save their homes will help these ancient mammals survive for many more millions of years.

Words to Know

burrow—a shelter dug in the ground

canine teeth—sharp fangs behind an insectivore's incisors that help tear up its prey

cheek teeth—an insectivore's back teeth used to chew food

class—a group of creatures within a phylum that share certain characteristics

family—a group of creatures within an order that share certain characteristics

genus (plural **genera**)—a group of creatures within a family that share certain characteristics

gland—an organ in the body that produces and releases a liquid

habitat—the environment where an animal lives and grows

incisor—a front tooth used for gnawing and cutting

kingdom—one of the five divisions into which all living things are placed: the animal kingdom, the plant kingdom, the fungus kingdom, the moneran kingdom, and the protist kingdom

larva (plural **larvae**)—the first stage of development for insects and some other kinds of animals

litter—a group of young mammals born at the same time to the same mother

mammal—an animal that has a backbone and feeds its young with mother's milk

mollusk—a soft-bodied animal that has no bones, such as an oyster, clam, or scallop

nutria—a large rodent that lives in South America

order—a group of creatures within a class that share certain characteristics

phylum (plural **phyla**)—a group of creatures within a kingdom that share certain characteristics

predator—an animal that hunts and eats other animals

prey—an animal that is hunted and eaten by other animals

saliva—a mixture of water and chemicals in the mouths; spit

species—a group of creatures within a genus that share certain characteristics. Members of a species can mate and produce young.

territory—the area where an animal lives, hunts, and has young

Learning More

Books

Baglio, Ben M. *Hedgehogs in the Hall.* New York, NY: Scholastic, 1998.

Garcia, Eulalia. *Moles: Champion Excavators.* Milwaukee, WI: Gareth Stevens, 1997.

Knight, Linday. *The Sierra Club Book of Small Mammals.* San Francisco: Sierra Club Juveniles, 1993.

Lilly, Kenneth. *Digger, the Story of a Mole in the Fall.* Orlando, FL: Raintree/Steck-Vaughn, 1997.

Web Sites

The Hedgehog Homepage
http://www.steveconrad.co.uk/hog/index.html
This site provides information about hedgehogs and includes a photo gallery and a page of links.

The Mammal Society
http://info.abdn.ac.uk/mammal/
This huge site has all kinds of information about all kinds of mammals. It provides fact sheets for moles, shrews, and hedgehogs in Great Britain.

The Mole Tunnel
http://www.moletunnel.net/
This site offers distribution maps, information about the general biology of moles, and links to other sites.

Index

About the Author

Sara Swan Miller has enjoyed working with children all her life, first as a Montessori nursery school teacher and later as an outdoor environmental educator at the Mohonk Preserve in New Paltz, New York. As the director of the preserve's school program, she has led hundreds of children on field trips and taught them the importance of appreciating and respecting the natural world.

Miller has written a number of children's books, including *Three Stories You Can Read to Your Cat*; *Three Stories You Can Read to Your Dog*; *Three More Stories You Can Read to Your Dog*; *What's in the Woods?: An Outdoor Activity Book*; *Oh, Cats of Camp Rabbitbone*; *Piggy in the Parlor and Other Tales*; *Better Than TV*; *Will You Sting Me? Will You Bite?: The Truth About Some Scary-Looking Insects*; five books on farm animals for the Children's Press True Books series; and several other books for the Animals in Order series.